Would You Like Some Water?

water

soda

tea

milk

lemonade

orange juice

hot chocolate

coffee

Would you like
some water?

Yes, please.

Would you like
some milk?

Yes, please.

Would you like
some coffee?

No, thank you!

Let's learn about Brazil.

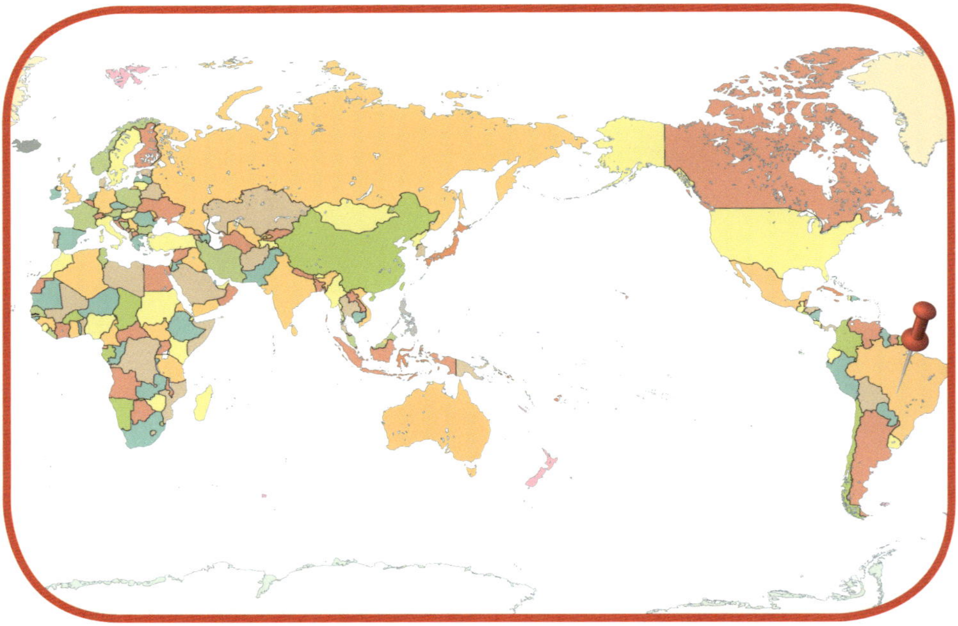

Flag of Brazil

Christ the Redeemer